Flowering Favorites

from Piece O' Cake Designs

BECKY GOLDSMITH & LINDA JENKINS

C&T PUBLISHING INC.

Text and artwork © 2003 Becky Goldsmith and Linda Jenkins
Artwork © 2003 C&T Publishing, Inc.
Editor-in-Chief: Darra Williamson
Editor: Lynn Koolish
Technical Editors: Gailen Runge, Frankie Kohler
Copyeditor/Proofreader: Eva Simoni Erb/Susan Nelsen
Cover Designer: Kristen Yenche
Design Director: Diane Pedersen
Book Designer: Staci Harpole, Cubic Design
Illustrators: Becky Goldsmith and Staci Harpole
Production Assistant: Lucas Mulks
Quilt Photography: Chris Marona unless otherwise noted
How-to Photography: Diane Pedersen and Lucas Mulks
Published by C&T Publishing, Inc., P.O. Box 1456, Lafayette, CA 94549

Front cover: *Flowering Vines* by Becky Goldsmith
Back cover: *The Anniversary Quilt* and *Love Apple Star* by Becky Goldsmith

Library of Congress Cataloging-in-Publication Data
Goldsmith, Becky.
   Flowering favorites from Piece O' Cake Designs / Becky Goldsmith
and Linda Jenkins. p. cm.
Includes bibliographical references and index.
   ISBN 1-57120-220-X (paper trade)
1. Appliqué--Patterns. 2. Quilting. 3. Flowers in art. I. Jenkins, Linda,
1943- II. Piece O'Cake Designs. III. Title.
   TT779.G6296 2003
   746.46'041--dc21
                              2003001067

Printed in China
10 9 8 7 6 5 4 3 2 1

Dedication

We all have a spark of creativity inside us. We dedicate this book to all quilters, who fan their own creative flames by the very act of making a quilt.

Acknowledgments

We offer a great big thank you to Lynn Koolish, our editor at C&T. Her hard work and expertise make *Flowering Favorites* a favorite of ours.

We *all* have Gailen Runge, our technical editor, to thank for checking the accuracy of the measurements and patterns you are about to use. Staci Harpole, this book's designer, has given *Flowering Favorites* its distinctive appearance. We love the cover that Kristen Yenche designed. Luke Mulks, the Production Assistant, made the production of this book go smoothly. We thank all of you for your excellent efforts.

Table of Contents

Basic Supplies

Fabric: All of the fabrics used in the quilts in this book are 100% cotton, unless otherwise noted.

Thread: Use cotton thread with cotton fabric. There are many brands to choose from. Work with different brands until you find the one that works best for you. We like both 50 weight DMC machine embroidery thread and Mettler 60 weight machine embroidery thread.

Batting: We prefer cotton batting. Our favorite is Hobbs Organic Cotton Batting.

Needles for hand appliqué: We use a size 11 Hemming & Son milliner needle. There are many good needles. Find the one that fits *your* hand.

Pins: Use ½" sequin pins to pin your appliqué pieces in place. Use larger flower-head pins to hold the positioning overlay in place.

Fusible web: If you prefer to fuse and machine stitch your appliqué, use a paper-backed fusible web. For cotton, use a light- or medium-weight fusible. Choose the one you like best and follow the directions on the package.

Non-stick pressing sheet: If you are doing fusible appliqué, a non-stick pressing sheet will protect your iron and ironing board.

Scissors: Use embroidery-size scissors for both paper and fabric. Small, sharp scissors are better for intricate cutting.

Rotary cutter, mat, and acrylic ruler: When trimming blocks to size and cutting borders, rotary cutting tools will give you the best results.

Marking pencils: We use either a General's charcoal white chalk pencil or a Quilter's Ultimate mechanical pencil to draw around templates onto the fabric.

Permanent markers: To make the positioning overlay, an ultra-fine-point Sharpie marker works best on the upholstery vinyl.

Clear upholstery vinyl: Use 54"-wide clear medium-weight upholstery vinyl to make the positioning overlay. You can usually find it in stores that carry upholstery fabric.

Clear heavy-weight self-laminating sheets: Use these sheets to make templates. You can find them at most office supply stores and sometimes at warehouse markets. If you can't find the laminate, use clear Contac paper.

Sandpaper board: When tracing templates onto fabric, place the fabric on the sandpaper side of the board. Then place the template on the fabric. You'll love the way the sandpaper holds the fabric in place when you trace.

Appliqué Supplies

Wooden toothpick: Use a round toothpick to help turn under the turn-under allowance at points and curves. Wood has a texture that grabs and holds. We like the round wooden toothpicks with carved ends that you can find at a Cracker Barrel restaurant or an Asian grocery store.

Full-spectrum work light: These lamps give off a bright and natural light. A floor lamp is particularly nice as you can position it over your shoulder. Appliqué is so much easier when you can see what you are doing.

Vellum or translucent foundation paper: We like to use vellum for paper piecing and string piecing. It is easy to see through and provides a stable foundation.

Cotton quilting gloves: These gloves make it easier to hold on to the quilt during machine quilting.

For Your Information

Fabric Preparation

Cotton has withstood the test of time and is easy to work with. We prewash our fabric before using it. This is a good way to test for colorfastness. Also, if the fabric is going to shrink, it does so before it is sewn into the quilt. The fabric is easier to work with, and smells and feels better if it is prewashed.

About our Fabric Requirements

Cotton fabric is usually 40" to 44" off the bolt. To be safe, we calculate our fabric requirements based on a 40" width.

Use the fabric requirements for each quilt as a guide, but remember that the yardage amounts will vary depending on how many fabrics you use and the sizes of the pieces you cut. Our measurements allow for both fabric shrinkage and a few errors in cutting.

Seam Allowances

All piecing is designed with $\frac{1}{4}$" seam allowances. Be accurate in your piecing so that your quilt tops will fit together properly.

The cutting instructions in this book are mathematically correct. However, variations in the finished size of your quilt top can result from slight differences in seam allowances and the amount of piecing. The measurements provided should be very close to your actual quilt size, but you should always measure **your** quilt and cut sashings and borders to fit.

Before You Start

If you're new to Piece O' Cake Designs appliqué techniques, read through the General Appliqué Instructions and Special Techniques starting on page 46.

Briar Rose

Made by Becky Goldsmith, 2001

Finished block size: 16" x 16"

Finished quilt size: 57" x 57"

There's a story that goes with this quilt. Becky was setting the interior of this quilt top together one evening. She was in a hurry to go watch a movie with her family. The quilt top was going together really well when she heard a very bad noise.

Guess where she used to keep her paper shredder? You guessed it—next to her sewing machine table. You know what that bad noise was. The shredder was eating the corner of the quilt top. It was not a pretty sight. There were tears. ▶

Materials

Light background print: 5 ½ yards

Red multicolor stripe (Sawtooth sashing, circles, leaves in border, binding): 2 ¼ yards

Brown bias stems: ⅝ yard

Red tone-on-tone (flowers, sashing, leaves in border): 1 ¼ yards

Yellow-green stripe (flower center): ⅓ yard

Blue/purple plaid (flower center, sashing corners, leaves in border): ½ yard

Green print and plaid leaves: a variety of fabrics to total 1 ¾ yards

Backing and sleeve: 3 ⅞ yards

Batting: 61" x 61"

⅜" bias bar (optional)

Vellum for paper piecing (Refer to Resources on page 64 for sources of vellum.)

▶ *There were some words. (Her son, Jeff, later told her that he didn't know she knew those words!) This quilt was very nearly named "Shredder."*

The shredder ate some of the pieced sashing and the corner of one of the appliqué blocks. It didn't eat much of the appliqué—the edge of a flower and leaf tip. Under some circumstances, if this happened to you, you might be tempted to give up. But you know what? It really didn't take that long to fix the mistake. It took Becky about four hours.

So, there are two morals here. The first, obviously, is to keep your shredder away from your sewing machine. The second is to not give in to despair. Take a deep breath, try to remain calm, and work your way through a mistake. There are very few things that can't be fixed.

Cutting

Light background print fabric
Outer borders: Cut 4 strips lengthwise 7" x 49".
Sawtooth sashing: Cut 18 strips 3" x 40", then cut into 448 rectangles 1 ½" x 3".
Block background: Cut 4 squares 18" x 18".
Corner squares: Cut 8 squares 3" x 3".

Red multicolor stripe fabric
Sawtooth sashing: Cut 17 strips 3" x 40", then cut into 432 rectangles 1 ½" x 3".
Binding: Cut 1 square 26" x 26" to make 2 ½"-wide continuous bias binding. (Refer to pages 56–57 for instructions.)

Brown fabric
Bias stems: Cut 1 square 20" x 20" to make 1 ½"-wide continuous bias. Make the finished bias stem ⅜" wide. (Refer to pages 58–59 for instructions.)
* *If you are using fusible web for machine appliqué, refer to Making Fusible Bias Stems on page 59.*

Red tone-on-tone fabric
Red sashing: Cut lengthwise:
   A. 2 strips 1 ½" x 20 ½" for the sashing between blocks
   B. 3 strips 1 ½" x 41 ½" for sashing between rows
   C. 2 strips 1 ½" x 43 ½" for side sashing.
Corner squares: Cut 8 squares 3" x 3".

Blue/purple plaid fabric
Sashing corners: Cut 20 squares 2 ½" x 2 ½".

Cut fabric for appliqué as needed.

Assembly

Appliqué

The appliqué pattern for the block is on page 10. The patterns for the borders are at the back of the book on Pullout #1, side A and Pullout #2, side A. Refer to pages 46–51 for instructions on making the placement overlay and preparing the appliqué.

1. Appliqué the blocks and borders.

2. When the appliqué is complete, press the blocks and borders on the wrong side.

Appliqué Tips

Use the circle appliqué technique for the flower circles, and the cutaway appliqué technique for the flower stems. (Refer to pages 52–55 for instructions.)

For the vines in the borders, refer to Special Techniques on pages 56–59 for instructions on making continuous bias and bias stems for hand or fusible machine appliqué.

We prefer to pin, then baste the vines in place before doing the appliqué. The overlay for the vines is long, so pin it in place before beginning. Slide the vine in place, align it carefully, and pin a bit at a time.

Sawtooth Sashing

Paper-piecing patterns are on page 11. Each Unit #1 uses 1 beginning pattern, 1 ending pattern, and 1 middle pattern. Each Unit #2 uses 1 beginning pattern, 1 ending pattern, and 4 middle patterns.

1. Trace or photocopy onto vellum 20 beginnings and 20 endings (one of each for 16 Unit #1 and 4 Unit #2), and 32 middle pieces (one for each Unit #1 and 4 for each Unit #2). Tape the patterns together.

2. Paper piece the Sawtooth sashing. Refer to Paper Piecing on pages 61–62. Place the light fabrics on the triangles marked "L." Place the dark fabrics on the triangles marked "D."

Trim the Blocks and Borders

1. Trim each appliquéd block to 16 1/2" x 16 1/2".

2. Trim each border to 5 1/2" x 47 1/2" (2 3/4" from the center line).

Quilt Assembly

Refer to the Quilt Assembly Diagram.

All of the measurements given for blocks and borders depend on the use of an accurate 1/4" seam allowance and accurate trimming. Measure the quilt as you go, to make sure that the quilt is coming together well.

Outer Border Corner Squares

1. Sew the light print and red squares together in pairs. Press the seams toward the red squares.

2. Sew the pairs of squares together into Four-Patch corner blocks, nesting the seams. Press. Make 4.

Sashing and Border Assembly

Note the direction of the triangle points in the Sawtooth sashing when putting the quilt top together.

1. Sew the Unit #1 Sawtooth sashings to opposite sides of each of the 4 center blocks.

2. Sew the sashing corners to both ends of the remaining Unit #1 Sawtooth sashings.

3. Sew these Sawtooth sashings to the tops and bottoms of the blocks.

4. Sew the blocks and the short red sashings (A) together in rows.

5. Sew the rows together with the 3 horizontal red sashings (B).

6. Sew the side red sashings (C) to 2 Unit #2 Sawtooth sashings.

7. Sew these sashings to the sides of the quilt.

8. Sew the sashing corners to the ends of the remaining Unit #2 Sawtooth sashings.

9. Sew these sashings to the top and bottom of the quilt.

10. Sew the borders to the sides of the quilt.

11. Sew a Four-Patch border corner to each end of the top and bottom borders.

12. Sew the top and bottom borders to the quilt.

13. Gently remove the vellum from the Sawtooth sashing.

14. Finish the quilt. Refer to pages 52, 56–61 for instructions.

Quilt Assembly Diagram

Briar Rose
One-quarter of center block
Make 4 copies to complete the block.
Full size, don't enlarge.

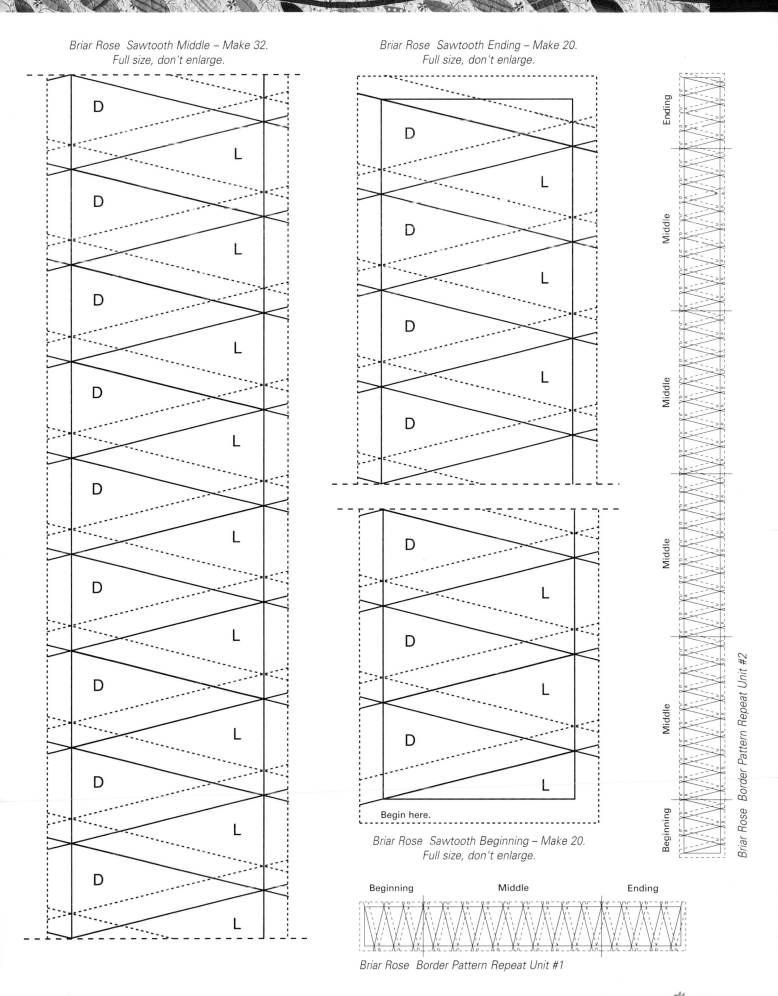

Briar Rose Sawtooth Middle – Make 32.
Full size, don't enlarge.

Briar Rose Sawtooth Ending – Make 20.
Full size, don't enlarge.

Briar Rose Sawtooth Beginning – Make 20.
Full size, don't enlarge.

Begin here.

Beginning   Middle   Ending

Briar Rose Border Pattern Repeat Unit #1

Briar Rose Border Pattern Repeat Unit #2

Ending

Middle

Middle

Middle

Middle

Beginning

Flowering Vines

Made by Becky Goldsmith, 2000
Finished quilt size: 65" x 76"

Happy! This quilt is happy! The colors are reminiscent of those used in the 1930s. The appliqué is easy. The pieced strips are sewn on foundation paper or vellum. It's a quick quilt to make. What could be better?

Appliqué quilts often have blocks in the center of the quilt surrounded by a vine border. This quilt is the reverse. The vine panels and string-pieced bars make up the center of the quilt. Flower blocks and short string-pieced units make up the border. We like to shake things up a bit!

Materials

Light tone-on-tone center strip backgrounds:
4 different fabrics, each at least 10" x 60", to total
1 ¾ yards

Light border blocks: A variety of fabrics to total 2
yards (Each piece must be at least 10" x 10".)

Multicolor string piecing: A variety of fabrics to total
2 ⅝ yards

Appliqué: A variety of fabrics

Brown bias stems: ⅔ yard

Blue inner border: ⅓ yard

Striped binding: ⅞ yard

Backing and sleeve: 4 ½ yards

Batting: 69" x 80"

⅜" bias bar (optional)

Vellum for string piecing (Refer to Resources on page
64 for sources of vellum.)

Cutting

Light tone-on-tone fabrics
Center strip backgrounds: Cut 4 strips lengthwise 10" x 60".

Light fabrics
Outer border block backgrounds: Cut 22 squares 10" x 10".

Multicolor fabrics
String piecing:
    Cut 10 strips 1" x width of fabric.
    Cut 11 strips 1 ½" x width of fabric.
    Cut 12 strips 2" x width of fabric.
    Cut 8 strips 2 ½" x width of fabric.
    Cut 7 strips 3" x width of fabric.

Brown fabric
Bias stems: Cut 1 square 22" x 22" to make 1 ½"-wide
    continuous bias. Make the finished bias stem ⅜" wide.
    (Refer to pages 58–59 for instructions.)
* If you are using fusible web for machine appliqué, refer to
Making Fusible Bias Stems on page 59.

Blue fabric
Inner border: Cut 6 strips 1 ½" x width of fabric, sew
together end to end, and cut:
    2 strips 1 ½" x 47 ½" for the top and bottom
      inner borders
    2 strips 1 ½" x 60 ½" for the side inner borders.

Striped fabric
Binding: Cut 1 square 30" x 30" to make 2 ½"-wide
    continuous binding. (Refer to pages 56–57 for
    instructions.)

Cut fabric for appliqué as needed.

Assembly

Appliqué

The appliqué patterns are at the back of the book on Pullout #1, sides A and B. Refer to pages 46–51 for instructions on making the placement overlays and preparing the appliqué.

1. Appliqué the vines. Refer to Special Techniques on pages 56–59 for instructions on making *continuous bias* and *bias stems* for hand or fusible machine appliqué. Make 2 of Panel 1, and 2 of Panel 2.

Vine Appliqué Tip

We prefer to pin, then baste the vines in place before doing the appliqué. The overlay for the vines is long, so pin it in place before beginning. Slide the vine in place, align it carefully, and pin a bit at a time. Leave a little extra vine where it goes under the flowers; you can trim it before you appliqué the flowers in place.

2. Appliqué the flowers and leaves on the strips and the blocks. There are 4 leaf shapes and 2 flowers (large and small) that are repeated throughout this pattern. Use 1 flower and 3 leaves for each outer border block.

Make 22 blocks. To be sure the appliqué is properly placed, make an 8" x 8" placement overlay. When you arrange the flower and leaves

on each block, center the overlay on the fabric and make sure that all appliqué is within ¹/₂" of the outer edge.

Flower Appliqué Tip

The flowers are easier to assemble "off the block," that is, before they are attached to the quilt. If you are doing machine appliqué with fusible web, follow the appliqué order as shown on the patterns, otherwise use the following directions.

Assemble the Flowers Off the Block for Hand Appliqué

Work from the top down when assembling these flowers. For the small flower:

1. *Sew appliqué piece #10 to a larger piece of the #9 fabric.*

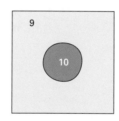

2. *Place template #9 over the #10 appliqué piece you just sewed down and trace around the template. Cut out the #9/10 unit, adding a ³/₁₆" turn-under allowance.*

3. Sew the combined #9/10 unit to a bigger piece of the #8 fabric.

4. Place the #8 template over the work, trace around it, and cut it out.

5. The entire flower is ready to sew to a block or center strip.

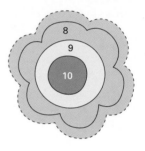

For the large flower, use appliqué pieces #5, #6, and #7, and follow the same instructions to assemble the flowers off the block.

3. When the appliqué is complete, press the blocks and strips on the wrong side.

String Piecing

String Piecing on Vellum

We like to string piece on top of vellum; you can use regular paper if you prefer. The vellum or paper gives these units stability.

- *Use long pieces of vellum from a roll, or tape pieces of vellum together to get the needed length.*

- *When sewing, use a large needle (size 90/14) in the sewing machine, and sew using a shorter-than-usual stitch length: 18–20 stitches per inch, or 1.5–1.8 on some machines. This will make the vellum easier to remove later.*

- *Leave the vellum on the strips until the quilt top is complete.*

1. Prepare the vellum for string piecing:

- For the center units, prepare 5 strips 3 1/2" x 58 1/2".

- For the wide border-corner units, prepare 8 strips 4 1/2" x 8 1/2".

- For the standard border units, prepare 14 strips 3 1/2" x 8 1/2".

2. Draw a line 1/4" from each cut edge on each strip of vellum. This is the seamline that you will use when sewing the quilt together.

3. Randomly select and cut the 1" to 3" multicolor strips to the needed width for each vellum foundation. Don't plan the size or color placement too carefully, so the strips will have a scrappy look.

Sewing Layers of Fabric

Use a walking or even-feed foot to keep both layers of fabric even, especially when sewing on vellum.

4. With the drawn side of the vellum face down, start at one end of the vellum and place 2 fabric strips, right sides together, on top of the vellum. Pin or hold the fabric strips to the vellum. Sew these 2 fabric strips to the vellum with a 1/4" seam allowance as shown. Sew all the way across the vellum.

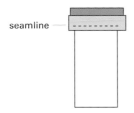

5. Press open.

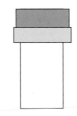

6. Place another fabric strip in position. Sew it down and press it open. Continue in this manner until the vellum is covered with strips. If you have trouble keeping the seamlines straight (and if this bothers you), use a ruler to draw some straight lines on the vellum to use as sewing guides.

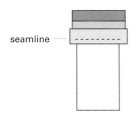

7. Place each unit on the cutting mat, vellum side up. Use a ruler and rotary cutter to cut away any fabric that extends past the edge of the vellum.

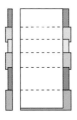

Trim the Blocks and Panels

1. Trim the border blocks to 8 1/2" x 8 1/2".

2. Trim the panels to 8 1/2" x 58 1/2" (4 1/4" from center line).

Quilt Assembly

Refer to the Quilt Assembly Diagram.

When sewing the blue inner borders, press the seam allowances toward the border after each step. When sewing the outer borders, press the seam allowance toward the inner border after each step.

1. Sew the appliquéd panels and the long string-pieced strips together to form the center of the quilt.

2. Press the seam allowance toward the appliquéd panels.

3. Sew the top and bottom inner borders to the quilt.

4. Sew the side inner borders to the quilt.

5. Sew the border squares and short string-pieced strips together to form the outer borders as shown.

6. Sew the top and bottom outer borders to the quilt.

7. Sew the side outer borders to the quilt.

8. Gently remove the vellum from the string-pieced strips.

9. Finish the quilt. Refer to pages 52, 56–61 for instructions.

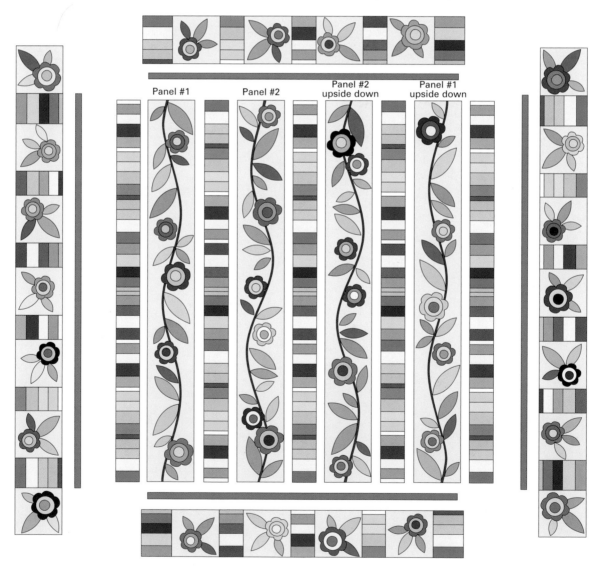

Panel #1   Panel #2   Panel #2 upside down   Panel #1 upside down

Quilt Assembly Diagram

Thistles

Made by Becky Goldsmith, 1997

Finished block size: 24" x 24"

Finished quilt size: 71 1/2" x 71 1/2"

Blocks set on point have energy. These spiky flowers enhance that energy. The pieced backgrounds create a texture that grounds the flowers but does not overpower them. When choosing your backgrounds, remember to keep the fabrics similar in color, value, and texture. Audition the backgrounds on your design wall before you piece them together. ▶

▶ *Would you like to know a secret? This quilt was designed with a slightly wider border. But the only fabric that worked—the perfect fabric—was one that Becky had had in her stash for several years. Nothing at the quilt shops even came close to working. She only had ½ yard of the perfect fabric so the border got narrower. This is why quilters must have good stashes— you just never know what you're going to need later.*

Materials

Yellow-gold backgrounds: A variety of fabrics to total 5 yards

Appliqué: A variety of fabrics to total 2 ¼ yards of rose/reds and purples and 2 ¾ yards of greens

Red inner border: ⅓ yard

Multicolor outer border: ½ yard

Purple binding or cording: ⅞ yard

Backing and sleeve: 4 ⅝ yards

Batting: 76" x 76"

³/₁₆" cording: 8 ½ yards (optional)

Fabric Selection Tips

When selecting fabrics, choose background colors that complement the appliqué and do not compete with it. We chose a wide variety of yellow-golds of similar value and scale for our sunny background. The more fabrics you use in the appliqué, the more vibrant this quilt will look. For the leaves and stems, choose a variety of greens from medium to dark, from blue-greens to true greens to yellow-greens. For the flowers and center stars, choose a variety of purples from red-purples to blue-purples. Remember to keep a strong contrast with the background.

Cutting

Yellow-gold fabrics
Background:
    Cut 24 squares 6 ½" x 6 ½".
    Cut 64 rectangles 6 ½" x 7 ½".
    Cut 24 squares 7 ½" x 7 ½".
    Cut 8 squares 10" x 10", then cut each square diagonally twice, to yield 32 triangles.

Red fabric
Inner border: Cut 8 strips 1" x width of fabric. Sew pairs of strips end to end, center seams, and trim each pair to 80".

Multicolor fabric
Outer border: Cut 8 strips 1 ¾" x width of fabric. Sew pairs of strips end to end, center seams, and trim each pair to 80".

Purple Fabric
Binding or cording: Cut 1 square 30" x 30" to make 2 ½"-wide continuous bias. (Refer to pages 56–57 for instructions.)

Cut fabric for appliqué as needed.

Assembly

Prepare the Backgrounds

Design Tip

Use a design wall to try out the placement of the background fabrics. When you are happy with the arrangement of the backgrounds, sew them together.

1. Piece the center background blocks as illustrated below. Lay out and sew the squares and rectangles carefully, so the seams align when you sew the block together.

7 ½" w x 7 ½" h	6 ½" w x 7 ½" h	6 ½" w x 7 ½" h	7 ½" w x 7 ½" h
6 ½" h x 7 ½" w	6 ½" h x 6 ½" w	6 ½" h x 6 ½" w	6 ½" h x 7 ½" w
6 ½" h x 7 ½" w	6 ½" h x 6 ½" w	6 ½" h x 6 ½" w	6 ½" h x 7 ½" w
7 ½" w x 7 ½" h	6 ½" w x 7 ½" h	6 ½" w x 7 ½" h	7 ½" w x 7 ½" h

2. Piece the corner triangles as illustrated below. Notice that the outer triangles will be a bit smaller than the rectangles they attach to. Position them as shown.

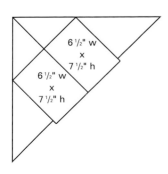

3. Piece the large triangles as shown.

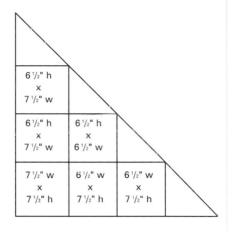

Appliqué

The appliqué patterns are on pages 22–23. They are reduced and need to be enlarged as noted on a photocopier.

Refer to pages 46–51 for instructions on making the placement overlay and preparing the appliqué.

Appliqué Tips

Use the cutaway appliqué technique for the stems, petals, and other small pieces; the two-part leaf technique for the leaves; and the circle appliqué and reverse appliqué techniques for the star center. (Refer to pages 52–56 for instructions.)

For the corner and large triangle backgrounds, roll up the outer points of the triangles and pin them to the body of the block to protect them while you appliqué.

1. Appliqué the thistles, leaves, and center stars to the center background blocks. Be sure to keep the stems on the true diagonal of the block. When the blocks are all pieced together, a stem that wanders will look out of place.

Center Star Appliqué Tips

1. Trace the #12 template onto the selected fabric and cut out, leaving at least 1" all around. Trace the #13 template onto the selected fabric and cut out, leaving at least 1" all around. Use the overlay to position piece #13 on piece #12. Pin and appliqué piece #13 to piece #12 using the cutaway appliqué technique.

2. Finger-press the circular edge of piece #13. Use the fold mark as a guide to trim the inner circle of piece #12 just inside the circular inner edge of piece #13. Cut out the inner circle of piece #13, leaving a scant $3/16$" turn-under allowance.

3. Use the overlay again to position the combined #12/13 piece. Use the reverse appliqué technique to stitch the inner circle to the block first, then use the cutaway appliqué technique to stitch the outer edges of the combined piece to the block.

4. Use the overlay again to position piece #14. Appliqué using the circle appliqué technique. Note that the thistle stems will show through the gap between pieces #12/13 and piece #14.

2. Appliqué the leaves to the corner triangles.

3. Appliqué the leaves and flowers to the large triangles.

4. When the appliqué is complete, press the blocks and triangles on the wrong side.

Trim the Blocks and Triangles

1. Trim the outer squares of each pieced center block by cutting 6 1/4" from the pieced seamline. The finished block size after final assembly is 6" x 6".

2. Trim the diagonal edge of the triangle 6 1/4" from the piecing line. Trim the straight edges 1/4" from the intersection of the seamlines. The finished size of the squares in the corner triangles after final assembly is 6" x 6".

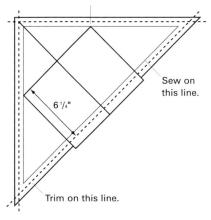

Trim this edge carefully 1/4" from this intersection.

6 1/4"

Sew on this line.

Trim on this line.

3. Trim the 2 straight sides of the triangles 6 1/4" from the piecing line. Trim the diagonal edge 1/4" from the intersection of the seam lines. The finished size of the squares in the large triangles after final assembly is 6" x 6".

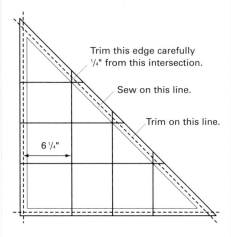

Trim this edge carefully 1/4" from this intersection.

Sew on this line.

Trim on this line.

6 1/4"

Quilt Assembly

Refer to the Quilt Assembly Diagram.

1. Sew the blocks, corner triangles, and large triangles together as shown in the Quilt Assembly Diagram.

2. Sew the inner and outer borders together, and press toward the outer border.

3. Place the quilt on a flat surface and measure from top to bottom through the center of the quilt. Use this measurement to mark the center points of the sides of the quilt. Fold the side borders in half lengthwise and mark the centers.

4. Pin the side borders to the quilt top, matching the center points of the quilt top edges and the center points of the side borders.

5. Stitch the borders to the sides of the quilt top. Start and stop stitching 1/4" in from the edge of the quilt top. Backstitch at the beginning and end of each seam. The border will extend beyond each edge— the excess will be trimmed after the miter is sewn. Press seams toward border.

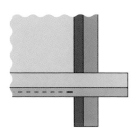

Stop stitching 1/4" from edge; backstitch.

6. Repeat with the top and bottom borders.

7. To create the miter, place 1 corner on the ironing board. Work with the quilt right side up and place 1 border on top of the adjacent border.

8. Fold the top border strip under itself so that it meets the edge of the outer border and forms a 45° angle. Press and pin the fold in place.

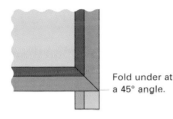

Fold under at a 45° angle.

9. Position a 90° triangle or a ruler over the corner to check that the corner is flat and square. When everything is in place, press the fold firmly.

Square corner.

10. Fold the center section of the top diagonally from the corner, right sides together, and align the long edges of the border strips. On the wrong side, place pins near the pressed fold in the corner, to secure the border strips.

11. Beginning at the inside corner, backstitch and then stitch along the fold toward the outside point. Be careful not to allow any stretching to occur. Backstitch at the end. Trim the excess border fabric to a $1/4$" seam allowance. Press the seam open. Repeat for the other 3 corners.

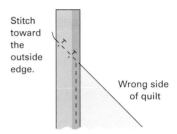

Stitch toward the outside edge.

Wrong side of quilt

12. Finish the quilt. Refer to pages 52, 56–61 for instructions.

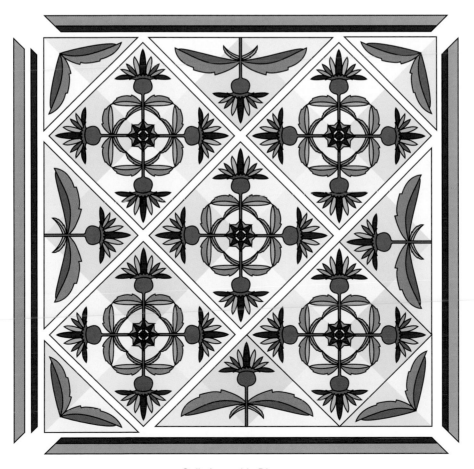

Quilt Assembly Diagram

Thistles
One-quarter of center block
Make 4 copies to complete the block.
Enlarge 158%.

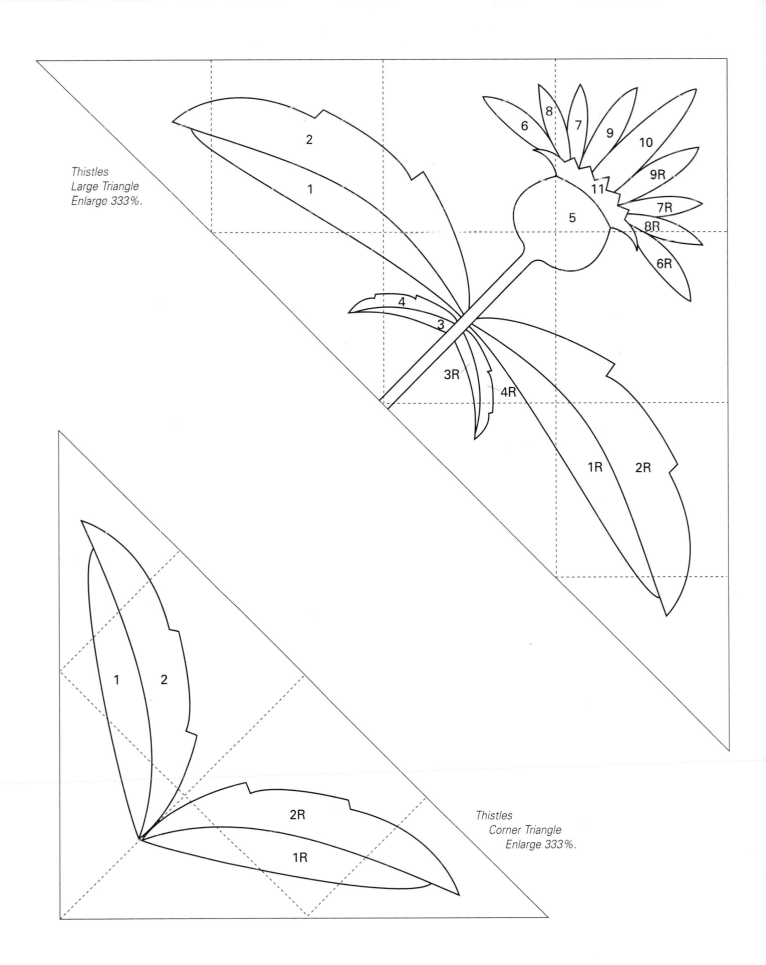

Thistles
Large Triangle
Enlarge 333%.

2

1

8

6

7

9

10

9R

11

5

7R

8R

6R

4

3

3R

4R

1R   2R

1   2

2R

1R

Thistles
Corner Triangle
Enlarge 333%.

Caribbean Dreams

Made by Linda Jenkins, 2001

Finished block size: 16" x 16"

Finished quilt size: 42" x 42"

This quilt combines Pennsylvania Dutch and folk art sensibilities to create a "contemporary folk" style. Linda used vibrant solids to strike just the right color chord; the embroidered accents dress up the flowers.

This quilt has a lot of circles. The more circles you appliqué, the better you will get. One circle all by itself had better be perfect, but the more circles you have together, the more "circular" they all look. Refer to the circle appliqué technique on pages 54–55 for more information on sewing lovely circles.

Materials

Light block background print: 1 ¼ yards

Light border background plaid: ⅞ yard

Appliqué: A large variety of scraps

Blue print inner border: ⅓ yard

Striped binding: ¾ yard

Backing and sleeve: 2 ⅝ yards

Batting: 46" x 46"

Embroidery floss

Cutting

Light print fabric
Block background: Cut 4 squares 18" x 18".
Border corner squares: Cut 4 squares 6" x 6".

Light plaid fabric
Outer borders: Cut 4 strips 6" x 36".

Blue print fabric
Inner border: Cut 2 strips 1 ½" x 32 ½" for the top and bottom. Cut 2 strips 1 ½" x 34 ½" for the sides.

Striped fabric
Binding: Cut 1 square 24" x 24" to make 2 ½"-wide continuous bias binding. (Refer to pages 56–57 for instructions.)

Cut fabric for appliqué as needed.

Assembly

Appliqué

The appliqué patterns are on pages 27–29. The center block pattern is reduced and needs to be enlarged by 216% on a photocopier.

Refer to pages 46–51 for instructions on making the placement overlay and preparing the appliqué.

1. Appliqué the blocks and borders. Embroider where desired.

2. When the appliqué and embroidery are complete, press the blocks and borders on the wrong side.

Appliqué Tips

Use the circle appliqué technique for the flower circles, and the cutaway appliqué technique for the flower stems and leaves. (Refer to pages 52–55 for instructions.) Use French knots and a straight embroidery stitch inside the flowers.

Trim the Blocks and Borders

1. Trim each block to 16 ½" x 16 ½".

2. Trim each border to 4 ½" x 34 ½" (2 ¼" from the center line).

3. Trim each border corner to 4 ½" x 4 ½".

Quilt Assembly

Refer to the Quilt Assembly Diagram.

1. Sew the squares together in pairs. Press the seams in each pair in alternate directions so the seams nest when the pairs are sewn together.

2. Sew the pairs together, nesting the seams. Press.

3. Appliqué the flower at the center of the quilt.

Sashing and Border Assembly

When sewing the inner borders, press the seam allowances toward the border after each step. When sewing the outer borders, press the seam allowance toward the inner border after each step.

1. Sew the top and bottom inner borders to the quilt.

2. Sew the side inner borders to the quilt.

3. Sew the side outer borders to the quilt.

4. Sew the corner blocks to each end of the top and bottom outer borders.

5. Sew the top and bottom outer borders to the quilt.

6. Finish the quilt. Refer to pages 52, 56–61 for instructions.

Quilt Assembly Diagram

Caribbean Dreams
Center Block
Enlarge 216%.

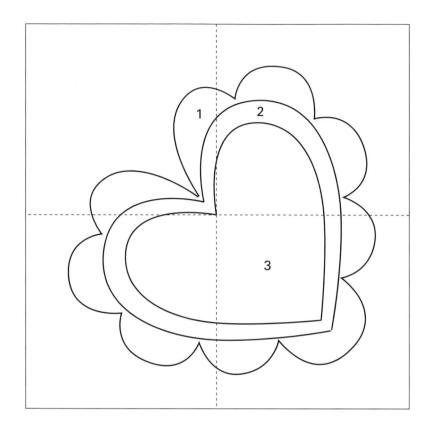

Caribbean Dreams
Border Corner Block
Full size, don't enlarge.

Caribbean Dreams
Center Flower
Full size, don't enlarge.

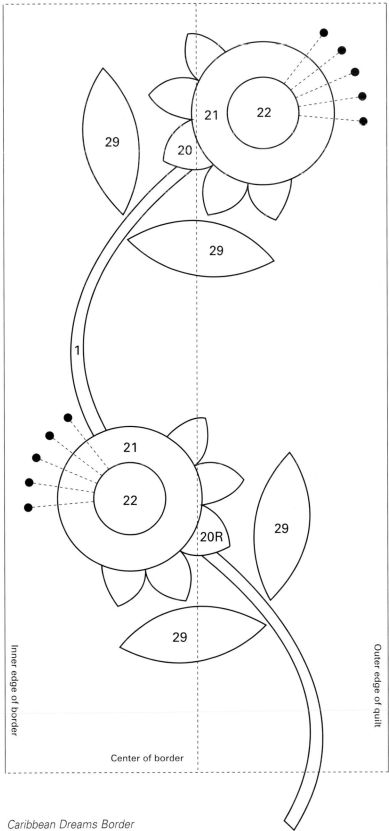

29

21 22

20

1

29

29

21

22

20R

29

29

Outer edge of quilt

Center of border

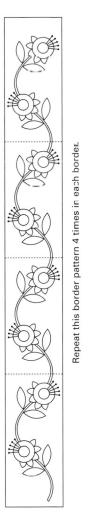

Repeat this border pattern 4 times in each border.

Caribbean Dreams
Border Pattern Repeat

Caribbean Dreams Border
Full size, don't enlarge.
Repeat this border pattern 4 times in each border (as shown at right). As you trace this pattern to draw your overlay, the dashed line between the 2 center sections will match up with the center dashed line. Cut the border fabric in 1 strip as indicated in Cutting on page 25.

Love Apple Star

Photo by Sharon Risedorph

Made by Becky Goldsmith, 1998

Finished quilt size: 63" x 63"

Appliqué blocks don't have to be square. Becky decided to appliqué diamonds in this quilt. And, just as in a pieced Lone Star, the repetition of the appliqué around the star creates a gentle circular momentum. The zigzags are easily made from continuous bias stem, as is the vine in the border. Use buttons, or appliqué the red berries in the zigzag.

Do read the instructions carefully. The appliqué is done on rectangular pieces of background fabric. Trim the blocks to their diamond shape after the appliqué is complete.

Materials

Light yellow diamonds: 1 3/4 yards

Dark yellow diamonds: 1 3/4 yards

Yellow border: 1 7/8 yards

Medium blue background: 2/3 yard

Yellow/blue plaid background: 1/4 yard

Floral background: 1 1/8 yards

Appliqué: A wide variety of small pieces of fabric

Dark green center stems: 3/4 yard

Green primary stem in border: 7/8 yard

Green branches in border: 7/8 yard

Dark blue zigzag: 1 yard

Striped binding or cording: 7/8 yard

Backing and sleeve: 4 yards

Batting: 67" x 67"

3/4" buttons: 44 for dips in zigzag

Embroidery floss: A variety of colors for flower stamens

Beads: A variety of colors for ends of flower stamens

3/16" cording: 7 1/2 yards (optional)

3/8" bias bar (optional)

Cutting

Light yellow fabric
Diamonds: Cut 4 rectangles 12" x 28".

Dark yellow fabric
Diamonds: Cut 4 rectangles 12" x 28".

Yellow fabric
Border background: Cut 4 strips lengthwise 10" x 62".

Medium blue fabric
Pieced corners: Cut 4 squares 10" x 10", then cut each
  square diagonally once to yield 8 triangles.
Pieced triangles: Cut 4 strips 5 1/2" x 11".

Yellow/blue plaid fabric
Pieced corners: Cut 8 strips 1 1/2" x 11 1/2".
Pieced triangles: Cut 4 strips 1 1/2" x 13".

Floral fabric
Pieced corners: Cut 8 strips 5 1/2" x 15 1/2".
Pieced triangles: Cut 4 strips 5 1/2" x 22".

Dark green fabric
Center stems: Cut 1 square 24" x 24" to make
  1 1/2"-wide continuous bias. Make the finished bias
  stem 3/8" wide. (Refer to pages 58–59 for instructions.)
* *If you are using fusible web for machine appliqué, refer
  to Making Fusible Bias Stems on page 59.*

Green stem fabric
Primary stem in border: Cut 1 square 26" x 26" to make
  1 1/2"-wide continuous bias. Make the finished bias
  stem 3/8" wide. (Refer to pages 58–59 for instructions.)
* *If you are using fusible web for machine appliqué, refer
  to Making Fusible Bias Stems on page 59.*

Green branch fabric
Branches in border: Cut 1 square 26" x 26" to make
  1 1/2"-wide continuous bias. Make the finished bias
  stem 3/8" wide. (Refer to pages 58–59 for instructions.)
* *If you are using fusible web for machine appliqué, refer
  to Making Fusible Bias Stems on page 59.*

Dark blue fabric
Zigzag: Cut 1 square 32" x 32" to make 1 1/2"-wide
  continuous bias. Make the finished bias stem
  3/8" wide. (Refer to pages 58–59 for instructions.)
* *If you are using fusible web for machine appliqué, refer
  to Making Fusible Bias Stems on page 59.*

Striped fabric
Binding or cording: Cut 1 square 27" x 27" to make
  2 1/2"-wide continuous bias binding. (Refer to pages
  56–57 for instructions.)

Cut fabric for appliqué as needed.

Assembly

Prepare the Backgrounds

Pieced Corners

1. Sew the medium blue triangle, the yellow/blue plaid strip, and the floral strip together as shown. Make 4 of unit A and 4 of unit B.

2. Cut along the diagonal line as shown.

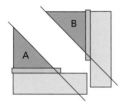

Cut on the diagonal lines.

3. Sew the 2 triangles together along the diagonal line to make 4 squares. These 4 squares are bigger than needed. Trim *after* the zigzag appliqué is complete.

Pieced Triangles

1. Sew the medium blue, yellow/blue plaid, and floral strips together as shown. Make 4. *Do not trim the diagonal edges of the triangle until the appliqué is complete.*

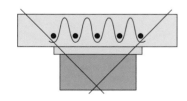

Trim after the appliqué is complete.

Appliqué

The appliqué patterns are at the back of the book on Pullout #1, side B and Pullout #2, sides A and B.

Refer to pages 46–51 for instructions on making the placement overlays and preparing the appliqué. **Note that the placement overlays for the diamonds, corners, and triangles are prepared a little differently than other overlays: Cut the upholstery vinyl and tissue paper as follows:**

- Diamonds: 11" x 25" rectangle
- Corners: 15" x 15" square
- Triangles: 11" x 21" rectangle

When drawing the overlays, be sure to include the appliqué design, the numbers, the seamlines, any grid lines, and the lines at the outer edges of the blocks. You will match the seamlines on the overlay to the seamlines in the blocks when you position the overlay.

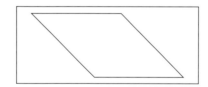

Layout of diamond for overlay.

Do not cut the overlays on the drawn edges. The extra vinyl will help prevent them from stretching. The overlays will be used to cut the blocks to size when the appliqué is complete.

Refer to pages 46–51 for instructions

Appliqué Tips

Press the fabric rectangles in half vertically and horizontally to establish the center grid. Press the assembled triangle backgrounds in half vertically; the seamlines provide the horizontal grid lines.

*Complete all the appliqué and pressing **before** cutting out the diamond, triangle, and square shapes.*

Use the circle appliqué technique for the smooth curves on the love apple flowers. (Refer to pages 54–55 for instructions.) For the vines, refer to Special Techniques on pages 56–59 for instructions on making continuous bias and bias stems for hand or fusible machine appliqué.

We prefer to pin, then baste the vines in place before doing the appliqué. Pin the overlay in place before beginning. Slide the vine in place, align it carefully, and pin a bit at a time. Leave a little extra vine where it goes under the flowers; you can trim it before you appliqué the flowers in place.

For each love apple flower, the larger background part of the flower is one template. The center piece can be appliquéd onto the background piece before adding the unit to the quilt.

Star Diamonds

1. Appliqué the stems, flowers, and leaves on the diamonds.

2. Embroider the stamens on the flowers.

3. When the appliqué and embroidery are complete, press the rectangles on the wrong side.

Pieced Corners

1. Make bias stems for the dark blue zigzag.

2. Position the overlay by lining up the drawn seamlines with the actual seamlines in the block. This will ensure that the zigzag is in the right place.

3. Appliqué the zigzag.

4. When the appliqué is complete, press the squares on the wrong side.

Pieced Triangles

1. Make bias stems for the dark blue zigzag.

2. Position the overlay by lining up the drawn seamlines with the actual seamlines in the block and the pressed vertical line. This will ensure that the zigzag is in the right place.

3. Appliqué the zigzag.

4. When the appliqué is complete, press the triangles on the wrong side.

Borders

1. Make bias stems for the green stems.

Appliqué Tips

Some of the appliqué cannot be completed until the border strips have been sewn to the body of the quilt (leaves #37, #38, and #39, and the ends of stems #4 and #5). Leave an extra 2" of stem at the ends of #4 and #5.

2. Appliqué the stems first and then the leaves.

3. When the appliqué is complete, press the borders on the wrong side.

Trim the Diamonds, Corners, Triangles, and Borders

1. Use the overlay as a cutting guide and cut out each star diamond. Position the overlay carefully on each block and pin in place. **Remember to add a ¼" seam allowance to each side of the diamond.** Do not cut the diamonds until you are ready to put the star together.

2. Trim each pieced corner to 14½" x 14½". (Refer to Pieced Triangles on page 32.) Make sure that the floral fabric behind the zigzag measures 4¾" wide. Use the positioning overlay as a cutting guide. **Be sure to add a ¼" seam allowance on all sides.**

3. Trim each pieced triangle. Make sure that the floral fabric behind the zigzag measures 4¾" wide. Use the positioning overlay as a cutting guide. **Be sure to add a ¼" seam allowance on all sides and cut to size.**

4. Trim each border strip to 8" x 56" (4" from the center line).

Quilt Assembly

Refer to the Quilt Assembly Diagram.

Be gentle with the bias edges on the diamonds and on the pieced triangles.

1. Sew together one pair of diamonds. Sew from the center out. Stop stitching ¼" away from the outside edge. Backstitch.

2. Inset a pieced corner. In two steps, sew from the inside corner out on both sides, starting ¼" away from the inside corner and sewing to the tip.

3. Press the seams toward the star.

4. Repeat Steps 1, 2, and 3 for the remaining 3 diamond pairs.

5. Sew together 2 diamond pairs to form one side of the star. Stop stitching ¼" away from the outside corner.

6. Inset 1 pieced triangle. In two steps, sew from the inside corner out on both sides, starting ¼" away from the inside corner and sewing to the tip.

7. Press the seams toward the star.

8. Repeat for the other 2 pairs to make the other side of the star.

9. Sew together the 2 sides of the star, insetting the last 2 pieced triangles.

10. Press the quilt top on the wrong side. Press the joining seams open to help reduce bulk.

11. Sew the first border strip to one side of the quilt. The end of this first border strip will extend 7 ¾" past the body of the quilt. Stop stitching ¼" away from the edge of the quilt.

12. Working counter-clockwise around the quilt, sew on the remaining border strips.

13. Complete the final corner by continuing the seam on the first border strip to the edge of the now-completed quilt top.

14. Finish the appliqué in the corners.

15. Press on the wrong side.

16. Finish the quilt. Refer to pages 52, 56–61 for instructions.

17. Sew on the beads at the ends of the flower stamens and the buttons in the dips of the zigzag.

Start first border strip here.

Quilt Assembly Diagram

The Anniversary Quilt

Made by Becky Goldsmith, 2000

Finished block size: 26" x 26"

Finished quilt size: 76" x 88"

The Anniversary Quilt was made to celebrate Becky and Steve's twentieth wedding anniversary. It is full of symbolic images special to quilters. The central rose in each block signifies love. The pomegranates denote a hope for abundance and fruitfulness. Oak leaves show bravery, and acorns signify longevity. The berries represent sweetness and security. Make this quilt for yourself or someone dear to you, and share with them its special meaning.

Materials

Light backgrounds: A variety of fabrics to total 7 3/8 yards

Colorful triangle strips: A variety of fabrics to total 1 yard

Appliqué: A variety of colorful fabrics to total 4 1/2 yards

Plaid bias vines: 3/4 yard

Multicolor binding or cording: 7/8 yard

Backing and sleeve: 5 2/3 yards

Batting: 80" x 92"

3/16" cording: 9 1/2 yards (optional)

3/8" bias bar (optional)

Vellum for paper piecing (Refer to Resources on page 64 for sources of vellum.)

Cutting

Light fabrics
Block backgrounds: Cut 16 squares 14" x 14".
Border backgrounds:
    Cut 12 rectangles 13 1/2" x 14".
    Cut 4 squares 14" x 14".
    Cut 4 rectangles 15 1/2" x 14".
    Cut 2 rectangles 12 1/2" x 14".
Triangle strip backgrounds: Cut 54 strips 2 1/2" x 7".

Colorful fabrics
Triangle strips: Cut 52 strips 2 1/2" x 7".

Plaid fabric
Bias vines: Cut 1 square 26" x 26" to make 1 1/2"-wide continuous bias. Make the finished bias stem 3/8" wide. (Refer to pages 58–59 for instructions.)
* If you are using fusible web for machine appliqué, refer to Making Fusible Bias Stems on page 59.

Multicolor fabric
Binding or cording: Cut 1 square 30" x 30" to make 2 1/2"-wide continuous bias binding. (Refer to pages 56–57 for instructions.)

Cut fabric for appliqué as needed.

Assembly

Prepare the Backgrounds

Design Tip

Use a design wall to try out the placement of the background fabrics for the blocks and borders. When you are happy with the arrangements, sew them together.

1. Piece together 4 background squares for each block.

2. Piece the top and bottom borders as shown.

These measurements are cut sizes, not finished sizes.

15 1/2" w x 14" h	13 1/2" w x 14" h	13 1/2" w x 14" h	15 1/2" w x 14" h

Top and bottom borders

3. Piece the side borders as shown.

14" h x 14" w	*These measurements are cut sizes, not finished sizes.*
13 1/2" h x 14" w	
13 1/2" h x 14" w	
12 1/2" h x 14" w	
13 1/2" h x 14" w	
13 1/2" h x 14" w	
14" h x 14" w	

Side borders

Appliqué

The appliqué pattern for the center flower is on page 40. The center flower pattern is reduced and needs to be enlarged by 340% on a photocopier. The patterns for the borders are on pages 41–42 and need to be enlarged as noted.

Refer to pages 46–51 for instructions on making the placement overlay and preparing the appliqué.

1. Appliqué the center blocks.

Appliqué Tips

Use the cutaway appliqué technique for the spirals, stems, and small leaves; and the circle appliqué technique for the berries. (Refer to pages 52–55 for instructions.)

The flower centers are easier to assemble "off the block," that is, before they are attached to the quilt. If you are doing machine appliqué with fusible web, cut a circle from the #6 fabric, then cut and fuse the #5 swirl on top. If you are doing hand appliqué, follow the instructions below.

Assemble the Centers Off the Block for Hand Appliqué

1. For each flower center, cut a 6" x 6" square of the fabric for the top swirl and a 6" x 6" square of the bottom fabric.

2. *Trace around template #6 onto the top swirl fabric. Finger-press the lines.*

3. *Place the top swirl fabric square (with the swirl traced on it) over the bottom swirl fabric square.*

4. *The dashed line is the cutting line. Cut, revealing the fabric below. Stitch, clipping curves where necessary.*

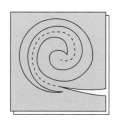

5. *Finish stitching the swirl. Use template #5 to trace the outer circle around the swirl. The stitching line is shown dashed. Cut out the swirl unit, adding a 3/16" turn-under allowance. The unit is ready to stitch in place.*

2. Appliqué the vines on the borders. Refer to Special Techniques on pages 56–59 for instructions on making *continuous bias* and *bias stems* for hand or fusible machine appliqué.

Vine Appliqué Tip

We prefer to pin, then baste the vines in place before doing the appliqué. The overlay for the vines is long, so pin it in place before beginning. Slide the vine in place, align it carefully, and pin a bit at a time. Leave a little extra vine where it goes under the leaves; you can trim it before you appliqué the flowers in place.

3. Appliqué the leaves and berries on the borders. Do not appliqué the leaves that are marked to be sewn after the borders are attached.

4. When the appliqué is complete, press the blocks and borders on the wrong side.

Leaf Appliqué Tips

For hand appliqué

1. *Cut a strip for each side of an oak leaf. For the majority of the leaves, cut strips 3³/₄" x 6¹/₂" for each side of the oak leaf. For the 4 large leaves, cut strips 4¹/₄" x 8" for each side of the oak leaf.*

2. *Sew the 2 strips together on the sewing machine. Press the seam allowance to the darker side.*

3. *Place the oak leaf template over the strips you sewed together. Match the center line on the leaf template to the seam line.*

4. *Trace around the template and cut out the leaf, adding a ³/₁₆" turn-under allowance.*

5. *Use the overlay to position the leaf on the border, and appliqué the leaf in place.*

For fusible appliqué

1. *Do not sew the 2 sides of the leaves together.*

2. *Iron fusible web to the back of all leaf fabrics.*

3. *Cut out each side of the leaves separately. Add a small allowance to 1 side of each leaf so they overlap at the centers.*

4. *Use the overlay for placement and fuse the leaves in place.*

Triangle Strips

The paper piecing patterns are on pages 43–45.

1. Copy onto vellum 1 beginning, 1 ending, and 4 middle sections for each of the 2 borders. Tape into two strips.

2. Paper piece the strips. Refer to Paper Piecing on pages 61–62. Use the background fabrics for the lighter triangles on the pattern, and the colorful fabrics for the darker triangles.

Trim the Blocks and Borders

1. Trim blocks to 26¹/₂" x 26¹/₂".

2. Trim the top and bottom borders to 12¹/₂" x 52¹/₂" (6¹/₄" from the center line). Trim the side borders to 12¹/₂" x 88¹/₂" (6¹/₄" from the center line).

Quilt Assembly

Refer to the Quilt Assembly Diagram.

When sewing the borders, press the seam allowances toward the border after each step.

1. Sew the center blocks together in pairs. Press the seams in alternate directions so they nest when sewn together. Sew the pairs of blocks together. Press.

2. Sew the triangle strips to the top and bottom of the 4 center blocks. Press toward the center blocks

3. Sew the top and bottom borders to the quilt. Press.

4. Sew the side borders to the quilt. Press.

5. Appliqué the last leaf in each corner.

6. Remove the vellum from the triangle strips.

7. Finish the quilt. (Refer to pages 52, 56–61 for instructions.)

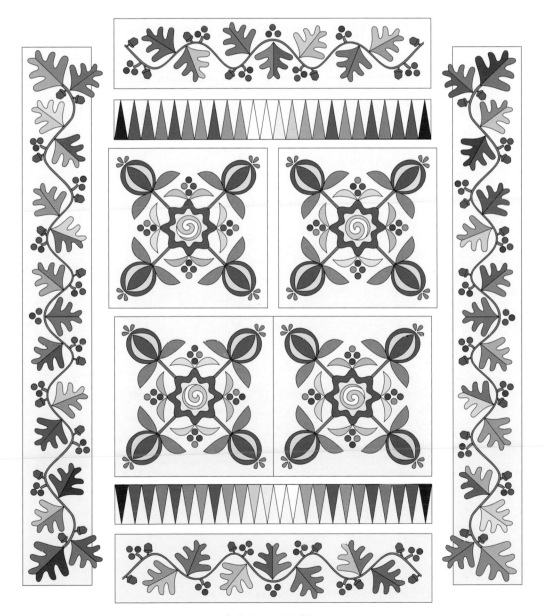

Quilt Assembly Diagram

The Anniversary Quilt
Enlarge 340%.

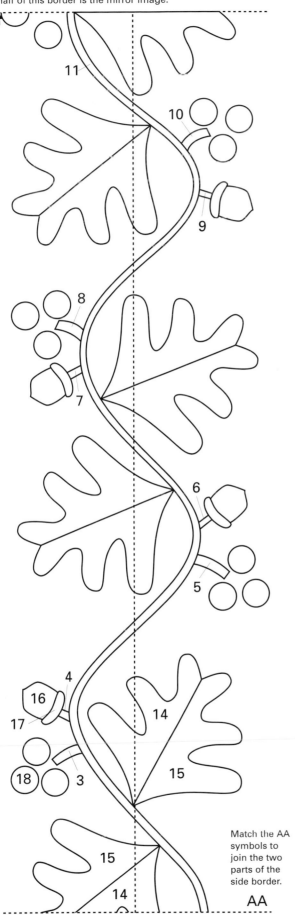

Center of the Side Outer Border. The other half of this border is the mirror image.

11

10

9

8

7

6

5

4

16

17

18   3

14

15

15

14

Match the AA symbols to join the two parts of the side border.

AA

The Anniversary Quilt
Side Outer Border
Enlarge 353%.

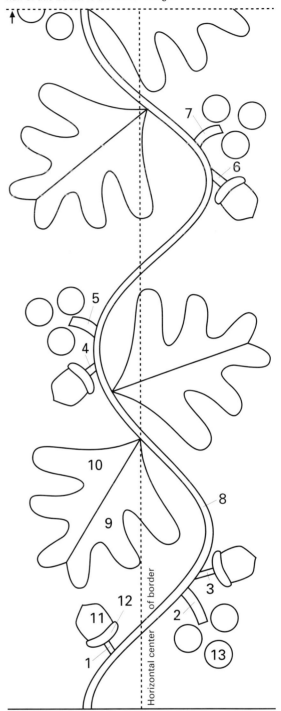

Center of the Top/Bottom Outer Border. The other half of this border is the mirror image.

7

6

5

4

10

9

8

11   12

1   2   3

13

Horizontal center of border

The Anniversary Quilt
Top/Bottom Outer Border
Enlarge 353%.

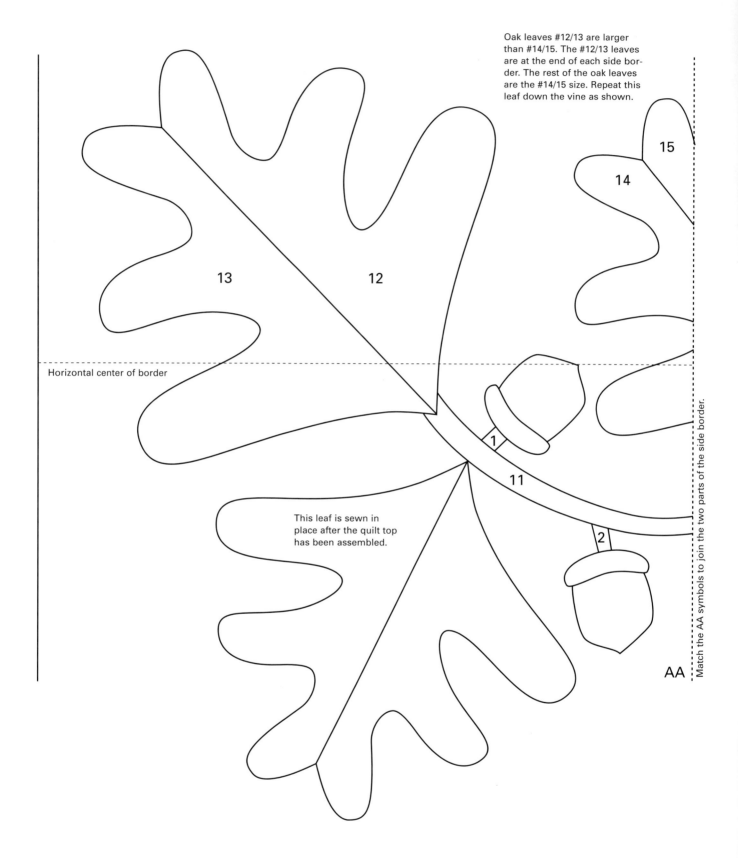

Oak leaves #12/13 are larger than #14/15. The #12/13 leaves are at the end of each side border. The rest of the oak leaves are the #14/15 size. Repeat this leaf down the vine as shown.

13

12

15

14

Horizontal center of border

11

1

2

This leaf is sewn in place after the quilt top has been assembled.

Match the AA symbols to join the two parts of the side border.

AA

The Anniversary Quilt
Side Outer Border
Enlarge 153%.

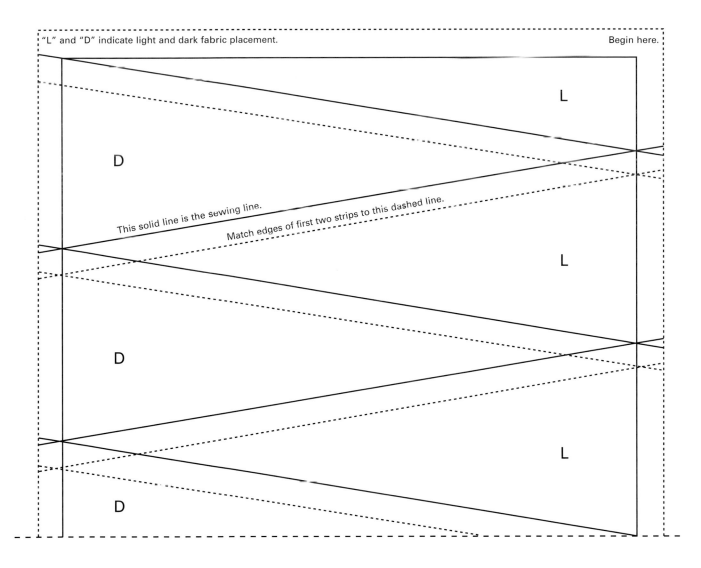

"L" and "D" indicate light and dark fabric placement.

Begin here.

L

D

This solid line is the sewing line.

Match edges of first two strips to this dashed line.

L

D

L

D

The Anniversary Quilt
Triangle Border Beginning
Make 2.
Full size, don't enlarge.

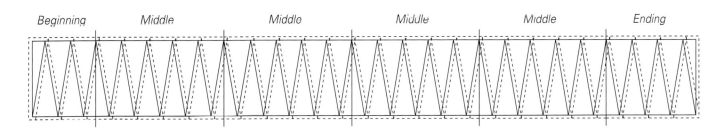

Beginning   Middle   Middle   Middle   Middle   Ending

The Anniversary Quilt
Border Pattern Repeat

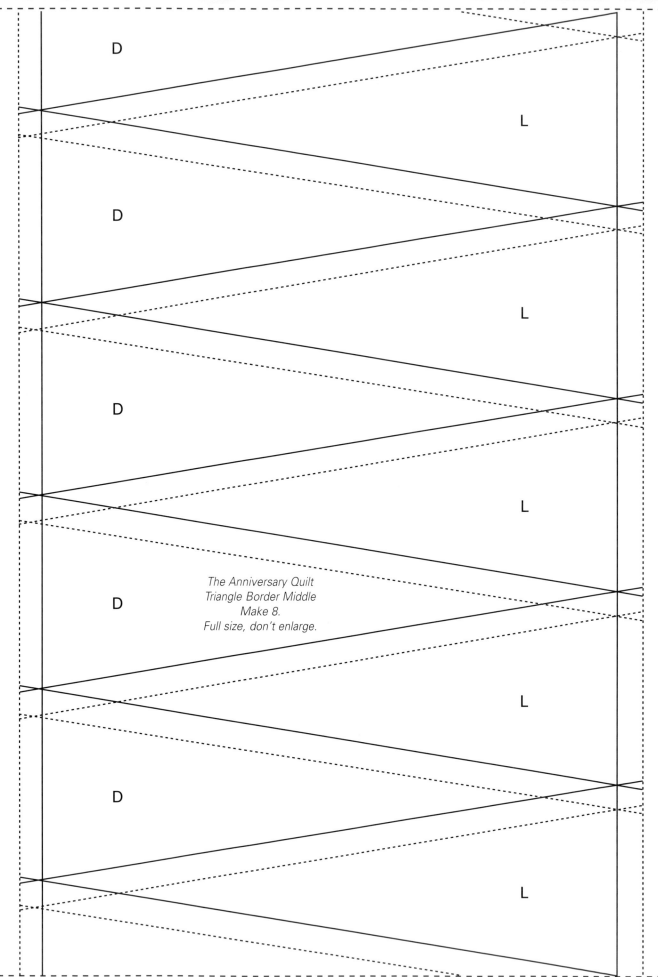

D

D

D

D

D

L

L

L

L

L

The Anniversary Quilt
Triangle Border Middle
Make 8.
Full size, don't enlarge.

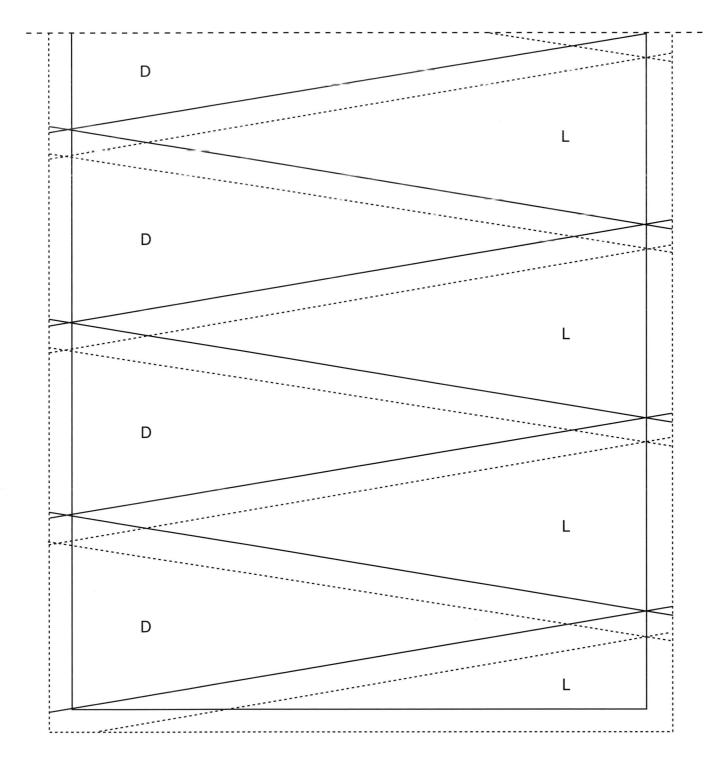

D

D

D

D

L

L

L

L

The Anniversary Quilt
Triangle Border Ending
Make 2.
Full size, don't enlarge.

General Appliqué Instructions

We have a great way to do appliqué using sturdy laminated appliqué templates and a clear vinyl positioning overlay that makes it a snap to position all the pieces. If you're new to Piece O' Cake Designs appliqué techniques, read through all of these instructions before beginning a project.

For a more complete description of all our appliqué techniques, refer to our book *The Appliqué Sampler*.

Preparing the Backgrounds for Appliqué

Always cut the background fabric larger than the size it will be when it is pieced into the quilt. The outer edges of the block can stretch and fray when you handle it while stitching. The appliqué can shift during stitching and cause the block to shrink slightly. For these reasons it is best to add 1" to all sides of the backgrounds when you cut them out. You will trim the blocks to size after the appliqué is complete.

1. Press each background block in half vertically and horizontally. This establishes a center grid in the background that will line up with the center grid on the positioning overlay. When the backgrounds are pieced, the seamlines are the grid lines, and you do not need to press creases for centering.

Press to create a centering grid.

Making the Appliqué Templates

Each appliqué shape requires a template, and we have a unique way to make templates that is both easy and accurate.

1. Use a photocopier to make 2-5 copies of each block. If the patterns need to be enlarged, make the enlargement as noted **before** making copies. Compare the copies with the original to be sure they are accurate.

2. Cut out groups of appliqué shapes from these copies. Leave a little paper allowance around each group. Where one shape overlaps another, cut the top shape from one copy and the bottom shape from another copy.

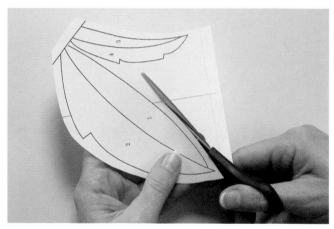

Cut out appliqué shapes.

3. Take a self-laminating sheet and place it shiny side down on the table. Peel off the paper backing, leaving the sticky side of the sheet facing up.

4. If you are doing hand appliqué, place the templates *drawn* side down on the self-laminating sheet. For fusible appliqué, place the **blank** side down. Take care when placing each template onto the laminate. Use more laminating sheets as necessary.

*Place appliqué shapes **drawn** side down on self-laminating sheets for hand appliqué.*

*Place appliqué shapes **blank** side down on self-laminating sheets for fusible appliqué.*

5. Cut out each individual shape. Try to split the drawn line—don't cut inside or outside of the line. Keep edges smooth and points sharp.

Cut out each template.

You'll notice how easy these templates are to cut out. That's the main reason we like this method. It is also true that a mechanical copy of the pattern is more accurate than hand tracing onto template plastic. As you use the templates, you will see that they are sturdy and hold up to repeated use.

Using the Templates for Hand Appliqué

Note that for our example we are using a two-part leaf. Refer to pages 55–56 for more information on making two-part leaves.

For needle-turn (hand) appliqué, the templates are used right side up on the right side of the fabric.

1. Place the appliqué fabric right side up on a sandpaper board.

2. Place the template right side up (shiny side up) on the fabric so that as many edges as possible are on the diagonal grain of the fabric. A bias edge is easier to turn under than one that is on the straight of grain. ▶

3. Trace around the template. The sandpaper will hold the fabric in place while you trace.

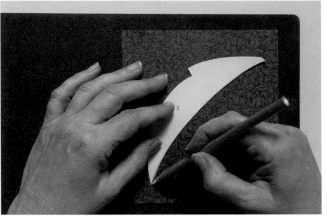

Place templates with as many edges as possible on the bias and trace around each template.

4. Cut out each piece, adding a ³/₁₆" turn-under allowance.

Cut out each piece adding a ³/₁₆" turn-under allowance.

5. Prepare the appliqué pieces for a block, and follow the instructions on pages 49–50 to make and use the positioning overlay.

Using the Templates for Fusible Appliqué

Note that for our example we are using a two-part leaf. Refer to pages 55–56 for more information on making two-part leaves.

For fusible appliqué, templates are used with the drawn side down on the wrong side of the fabric. Use a non-stick pressing cloth to protect the iron and ironing board.

1. Follow the instructions on the fusible web and iron it to the **wrong** side of the appliqué fabric. Do not peel off the paper backing.

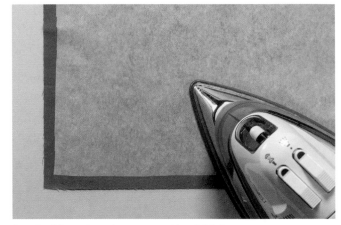

*Iron fusible web to the **wrong** side of fabric.*

2. Leave the fabric right side down. Place the template drawn side down (shiny laminate side up) and trace around it onto the paper backing of the fusible web.

Trace around template onto paper backing.

3. Cut out the appliqué pieces on the drawn line.

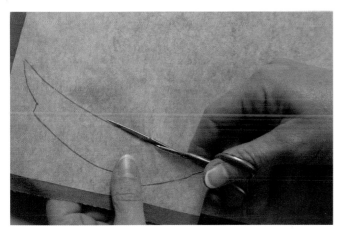

Cut out appliqué pieces on drawn line.

4. Prepare the appliqué pieces for a block, then follow the instructions below to make and use the positioning overlay.

Making the Positioning Overlay

The positioning overlay is a piece of clear upholstery vinyl that is used to position each appliqué piece accurately on the block. The overlay is easy to make and use, and it makes your projects portable.

1. Cut a piece of clear upholstery vinyl, with its tissue paper lining, to the finished size of each block. Set the tissue paper aside until you are ready to fold or store the overlay.

2. Make a copy of the patterns in this book to work from. Enlarge as directed. Tape pattern pieces together as needed.

3. Tape the copy of a pattern onto a table.

4. Tape the upholstery vinyl over the pattern. Use a ruler and an ultra fine point Sharpie marker to draw the pattern's horizontal and vertical center lines onto the vinyl.

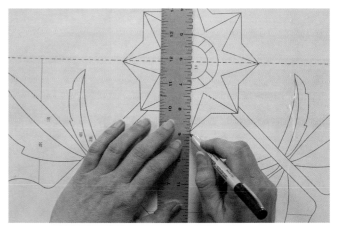

Tape vinyl over pattern and draw center lines.

5. Trace all the lines from the pattern accurately onto the vinyl. The numbers on the pattern indicate stitching sequence—include these numbers on the overlay.

Trace pattern onto the vinyl.

Using the Positioning Overlay for Hand Appliqué

1. Place the background right side up on the work surface.

2. Place the overlay right side up on top of the background.

3. Line up the center grid of the fabric or the seamlines with the center grid of the overlay.

4. Pin the overlay if necessary to keep it from shifting out of position.

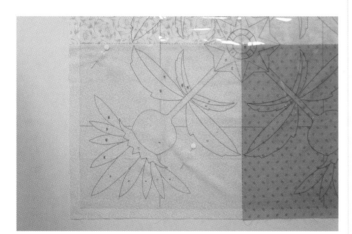

Place overlay on background and line up grids.

5. Before placing appliqué pieces on the block, finger-press the turn-under allowances. **This is a very important step.** As you finger-press, make sure that the drawn line is pressed to the back. You'll be amazed at how much easier this one step makes needle-turning the turn-under allowance.

Finger-press each piece with the drawn line to the back.

6. Place the first piece under the overlay but on top of the background. It is easy to tell when the appliqué pieces are in position under the overlay. As you work, finger-press and position one piece at a time. Be sure to follow the appliqué order.

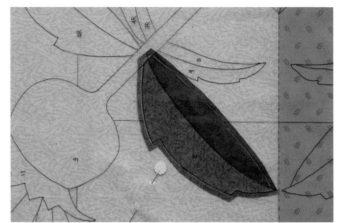

Use overlay to position appliqué pieces.

7. Fold the overlay back and pin the appliqué pieces in place using ¹/₂" sequin pins. We generally position and stitch only one or two pieces at a time. Remove the vinyl overlay before stitching.

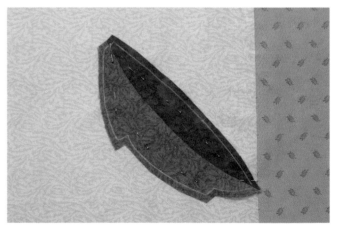

Pin appliqué piece in place.

8. Hand appliqué the pieces in place with an invisible stitch and matching thread.

9. When you are ready to put away the overlay, place the tissue paper over the drawn side before you fold it. The tissue paper keeps the lines from transferring from one part of the vinyl to another.

For Your Information

We don't trim the fabric behind our appliqué. We believe leaving the background intact makes the quilt stronger. And, should the quilt ever need to be repaired, it's easier if the background has not been cut.

Using the Positioning Overlay for Fusible Appliqué

1. Place the background right side up on the ironing board.

2. Place the overlay right side up on top of the background.

3. Line up the center grid of the fabric or the seam lines with the center grid of the overlay.

Place overlay on background and line up grids.

4. Peel off the paper backing from each appliqué piece.

5. Place the appliqué pieces right side up, under the overlay but on top of the background. Start with the #1 appliqué piece and follow the appliqué order. It is easy to tell when the appliqué pieces are in position under the overlay. You may be able to position several pieces at once.

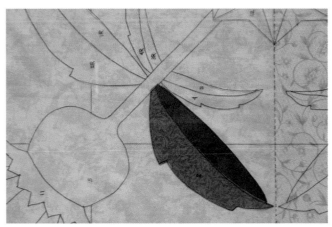

Use overlay to position appliqué pieces.

6. Carefully remove the overlay and iron the appliqué pieces in place. Be sure to follow the instructions for your brand of fusible web. Do not touch the overlay vinyl with the iron because the vinyl will melt.

Fuse appliqué pieces in place.

7. After fusing cotton fabric, we sew the raw edges of the fused appliqué on the sewing machine using a straight or blanket stitch and matching thread. As the quilts are used, the machine stitching keeps the edges secure.

Pressing and Trimming the Blocks

1. Press the blocks on the wrong side after the appliqué is complete. If the ironing surface is hard, place the blocks on a towel and the appliqué will not get flattened.

2. Carefully trim each block to size. Measure from the center out, and always make sure the design is properly aligned with the ruler before you cut off the excess fabric.

Finishing the Quilt

1. Assemble the quilt top following the instructions for each project.

2. Construct the back of the quilt, piecing as needed.

3. Place the backing right side down on a firm surface. Tape it down to keep it from moving around while you are basting.

4. Place the batting over the backing and pat out any wrinkles.

5. Center the quilt top right side up over the batting.

6. Baste the layers together.

7. Quilt by hand or machine.

8. Trim the outer edges, then finish them with continuous bias binding or cording. (Refer to pages 56–61.) Sew on any hard embellishments (buttons, beads, et cetera) now.

Making a Label and Sleeve

1. Make a hanging sleeve and attach it to the back of the quilt. Use fabric left over from the backing.

2. Make a label and sew it to the back of the quilt. Include information that you want people to know about the quilt: your name and address, the date, the fiber content of the quilt and batting, and if it was made for a special person or occasion.

Special Techniques

Cutaway Appliqué

The cutaway technique makes it much easier to stitch irregular, long, thin, or very small pieces. It is especially good to use for stars and stems.

1. Place the template on top of the selected fabric. Be sure to place the template on the fabric so that most of the edges will be on the diagonal grain of the fabric. Trace around the template.

2. Cut out the appliqué piece, leaving 1" or more of excess fabric around the traced shape. Be sure to leave fabric intact between star points, the "V" between branches, and so on.

3. Finger-press, making sure the drawn line is pressed to the back.

4. Note that this star (from *Thistles*) is stitched "off the block," that is, before it is attached to the quilt. For other cutaway pieces, use the vinyl overlay to position the appliqué piece on the block.

5. Place pins ¼" away from the edges that will be stitched. The position of the pin at a point is very important. This pin keeps the point in exactly the right

place. Place the pin ¼" away from, and parallel to, the first side of the point. The pin extends into the seam allowance, but you will remove it before you sew the second side of the point.

6. Begin cutting the excess fabric away from where you will start stitching, leaving a ³⁄₁₆" turn-under allowance. Never start at an inner or outer point.

7. Trim away more fabric as you sew. Clip inner curves and points as needed.

8. Remove the pins as you stitch the next side of the piece. Clip away excess fabric as necessary.

9. Continue until all sides of the appliqué piece are stitched.

Reverse Appliqué

Use reverse appliqué when you want to cut through one piece of fabric to reveal the fabric below it.

1. Place the template with the opening in it on top of the selected fabric. Be sure to place the template on the fabric so that most of the edges will be on the diagonal grain of the fabric. Trace around the template.

2. In most cases, you will cut out the appliqué piece leaving 1" or more of excess fabric around it. Don't cut out the opening yet, but finger-press it, making sure the drawn line is pressed to the back. In our example from *Thistles*, the appliqué pieces are already stitched to the block.

3. Position the appliqué piece on top of the fabric that will show through. Make sure that you leave the bottom fabric large enough so you can handle it easily. Pin the appliqué piece in place. Position the pins ¼" away from the edge that will be stitched first.

4. Cut inside the drawn line around the opening, leaving a ³/₁₆" turn-under allowance.

5. Clip any inner corners or curves as necessary and begin sewing. Never begin sewing at a point or corner.

6. Finish sewing the opening.

Circle Appliqué

When sewing outer curves and circles you can only control one stitch at a time. Use the needle or a wooden toothpick to smooth out any pleats that form. Remember, the more you practice, the better you'll get.

1. Trace circles onto the selected fabric. Cut out each circle, adding a ³/₁₆" turn-under allowance.

2. Finger-press the turn-under allowance, making sure the drawn line is pressed to the back.

3. Use the vinyl overlay to position the appliqué piece. Pin it in place. Use at least 2 pins to keep the circle from shifting.

4. Begin sewing. Turn under only enough turn-under allowance to take one or two stitches. If you turn under more, the appliqué will have flat spaces and points.

5. Use the tip of the needle to reach under the appliqué to spread open any folds and to smooth out any points.

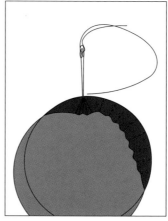
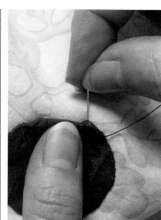

As seen from the back

6. To close the circle, turn under the last few stitches all at once. The circle will tend to flatten out.

7. Use the tip of the needle to smooth out the pleats in the turn-under allowance and to pull the flattened part of the circle into a more rounded shape. Finish stitching the circle.

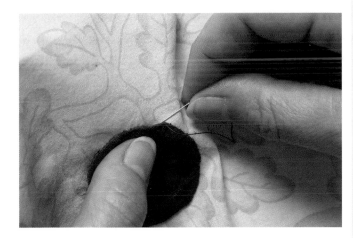

Two-Part Leaves

When you have a leaf that is made up of two parts, it is easer if you construct it before you sew it to the block. Remember to follow the stitching sequence indicated by the appliqué numbers. The appliqué piece with the higher number is sewn on top of the piece with the lower number. Follow the instructions carefully—don't trace or cut out the piece on the bottom until the top fabric has been sewn to it.

1. Select the two fabrics for the leaf. Trace around the template with the higher number onto the appropriate fabric, then cut it out adding a $^3/_{16}$" turn-under allowance.

2. Finger-press the vein side of the appliqué piece and pin it to the other leaf fabric. Sew the higher-numbered piece down along the leaf vein. Do not sew beyond the traced lines.

Sew along the leaf vein.

3. Place the lower-numbered template in position next to the sewn vein line. Trace around the outer edge to form the rest of the leaf.

Trace the rest of the leaf. ▶

4. Cut out the entire leaf, adding a ³/₁₆" turn-under allowance. On the side of the leaf where the fabric is doubled, turn the leaf over and trim at ³/₁₆" from the seam.

Cut out leaf adding ³/₁₆" turn-under allowance.

5. Sew the leaf as a unit to the block.

Making Continuous Bias

We find this method for making continuous bias to be particularly easy. A surprisingly small amount of fabric makes quite a bit of bias, and there is no waste. Use it for bias vines, as well as for bias binding. We show you how to master those tricky binding corners on page 57.

1. Start with a square of fabric and cut it in half diagonally.

2. Sew the two triangles together, right sides together, as shown. Be sure to sew the edges that are on the straight of grain. If you are using striped fabric, match the stripes. You may need to offset the fabric a little to make the stripes match.

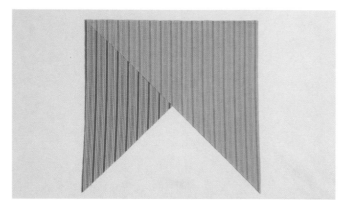

3. For bias for stems, press the seams to one side; otherwise press the seam allowances open. Cut the desired width into each side about 4" as shown.

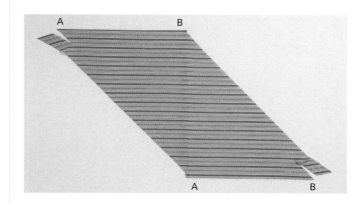

4. Match the A's and B's with the fabric right sides together. Pin and sew. Press the seam open.

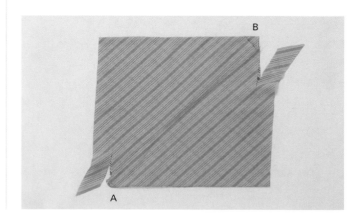

5. Use a rotary cutter and ruler to cut the continuous bias strip to the desired width

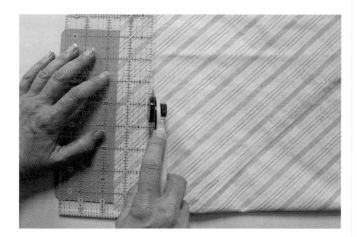

Cutting Tip for Continuous Bias

Try putting a small cutting mat on the end of the ironing board. Slide the tube of fabric over the mat. Use a ruler and rotary cutter to cut a long strip of continuous bias, rotating the tube of fabric as needed.

Cut using gentle pressure—if the ironing board is padded, the cutting surface may give if you press very hard.

Sewing Binding to the Quilt

1. Cut the first end of the binding at a 45° angle. Turn this end under ¼" and press.

2. Press the continuous binding strip in half lengthwise, wrong sides together.

3. With raw edges even, pin the binding to the edge of the quilt beginning a few inches away from a corner. Start sewing 6" from the beginning of the binding strip, using a ¼" seam allowance.

4. Stop ¼" away from the corner and backstitch several stitches.

5. Fold the binding straight up as shown. Note the 45° angle.

6. Fold the binding straight down and begin sewing the next side of the quilt.

7. Sew the binding to all sides of the quilt, following the process in steps 4-6 for the corners. Stop a few inches before you reach the beginning of the binding, but don't trim the excess binding yet.

8. Overlap the ends of the binding and cut the second end at a 90° angle. *Be sure to cut the binding long enough so the cut end is covered completely by the angled end.*

9. Slip the end that is cut at 90° into the angled end.

10. Pin the joined ends to the quilt and finish sewing the binding to the quilt.

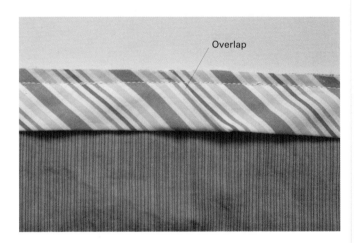

Overlap

11. Turn the binding to the back of the quilt, covering the raw edges. Hand stitch the folded edge of the binding to the back of the quilt.

Making Bias Stems

1. Make a continuous bias strip 1 ½" wide. (Refer to pages 56–57 for instructions.) Press the strip in half lengthwise with the wrong sides together.

2. Place the folded edge of the bias strip along the ³/₈" line on the seam guide of the sewing machine. Before you sew too far, insert the bias bar into the open end to make sure it fits. Sew the length of the bias strip.

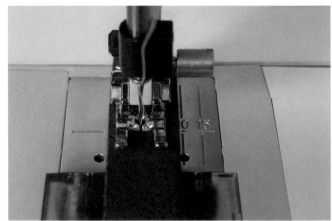

3. Trim away the excess fabric, leaving a very scant seam allowance.

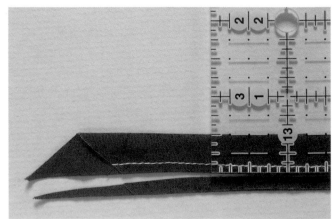

4. Insert the ³/₈" bias bar into the sewn bias tube. Shift the seam to the back of the bar and press it in place. Move the bias bar down the tube, pressing as you go.

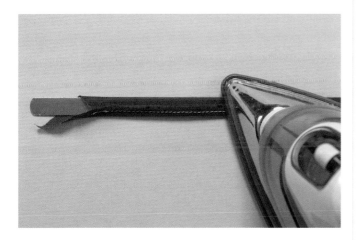

5. Hold up the finished bias stem. Notice that it curves more in one direction than the other. The side closest to the seamline makes the tighter curve. When possible, match this side of the bias stem to the concave side of the stem on the pattern.

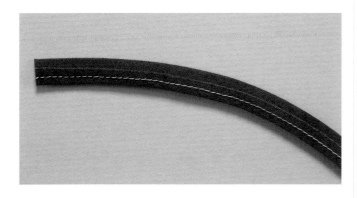

6. This technique can be used for any width bias stem.

Making Fusible Bias Stems

Here's the best way to make bias stems, if you prefer to do machine appliqué using fusible web.

1. Cut 6"-wide bias strips from the vine or stem fabric.

2. Iron 6"-wide strips of paper-backed fusible web to the back of the fabric.

3. Cut ³/₈"-wide strips for the stems or vines.

4. Peel away the paper backing and position stems on the block. Overlap the ends of the stems or vines as needed. When possible, place the end of the bias stem under a flower or leaf.

Making Cording

1. Make a continuous bias strip 1½" wide. (Refer to pages 56–57 for instructions.)

2. Trim one end of the strip so it is square.

3. Fold the bias strip in half lengthwise, wrong sides together. Press gently.

4. Fold under the trimmed end 1½", wrong sides together. Press.

5. Lay the cording down the lengthwise center of the wrong side of the bias strip, beginning 1" from the fold at the end.

6. Fold the bias fabric around the cording and stitch with a zipper foot and matching thread.

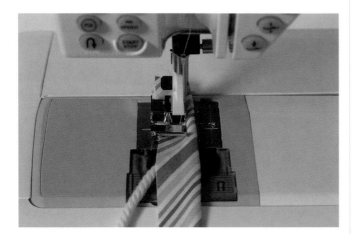

7. Trim the seam allowance to ¼", leaving 1 ½" at the beginning untrimmed.

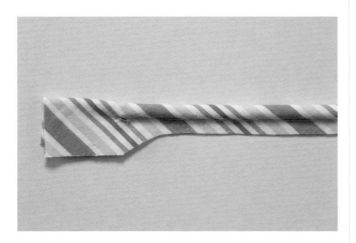

Applying the Cording

1. Apply the cording to the quilt top *before* layering and basting.Start in an inconspicuous place (not a corner). With right sides together and raw edges aligned, use a zipper foot to stitch the cording to the outer edge of the quilt top with a ¼" seam. Begin the stitching 1 ½" from the folded end of the cording. Round the corners slightly, being careful to make each corner the same.

2. When you have stitched all the way around the quilt top, cut the cording so it fits snugly into the folded opening at the beginning. The cord ends inside the bias fabric should just touch each other.

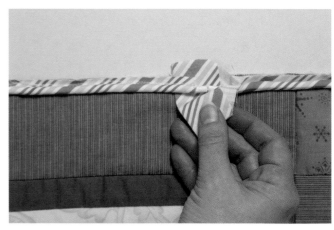

3. Finish stitching the cording to the quilt top.

4. Layer and baste the quilt. Turn the quilt right side down and trim the batting to the cording seamline.

5. Trim the quilt back even with the outer raw edge of the top ($\frac{1}{4}$" larger than the batting).

6. Turn the seam allowances from the top and cording over the edge of the batting.

7. Turn under the backing of the quilt to cover the raw edges and stitch invisibly.

Cording Tip

When sewing the cording to the quilt top, you need to plan ahead. If you are planning to do heavy quilting, you need to gently pull the cording a bit when you sew it on. The edges will look drawn-up, but this will be smoothed out because heavy quilting will also draw-up the quilt top. If you are planning to do light to moderate quilting, make sure you don't pull on the cording or on the top.

We recommend making a 14" test block. Apply the cording and quilt in the same manner as you would for the whole quilt. Look at the outer edges and see if they are smooth and flat.

Paper Piecing

Once you get used to it, paper piecing is an easy way to do very accurate piecing. You sew with the side of the paper with the printed lines facing up. Fabric is placed on the non-printed side.

We prefer using vellum instead of plain paper because it is easy to see through and provides a firm foundation. You can often find sheets of vellum at quilt stores or office and art supply stores, as well as on the internet. You can also find vellum on rolls at art and architecture supply stores. (See Resources on page 64.)

1. Photocopy or trace onto vellum the number of paper-piecing patterns needed for the project. Compare the copies to the original to be certain that you are getting accurate copies. Tape vellum end to end where necessary. Trim papers along outer edges of the patterns.

2. Sew the fabric to the vellum using a large needle (size 90/14) in the sewing machine, and sew using a shorter-than-usual stitch length: 18–20 stitches per inch or 1.5–1.8 on some machines. This results in tighter stitches that can't be pulled apart when you tear off the paper. ▶

3. Start sewing at the "Begin Here" on the pattern. Place the first two pieces of fabric right sides together on the unprinted side the vellum, as shown. Be sure that the wrong side of the first piece of fabric is next to the vellum. Line up the edges of the fabric with the **dashed line** on the paper. Sew on the **solid line**. Always sew with the drawn lines up and the fabric underneath and make sure you have a ¼" seam allowances.

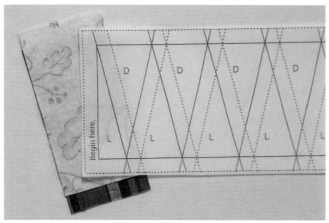

Sew with the paper on top and the fabric underneath.

4. Press open.

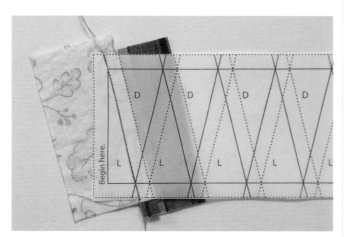

Press open.

5. Fold the paper back on the solid line and trim at ¼" from the seamline.

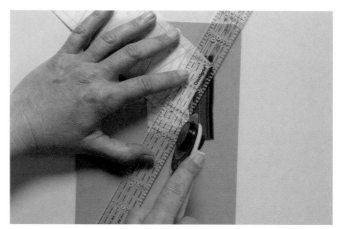

Trim excess fabric.

6. Sew the next strip, press open, and trim. Proceed in this manner until the entire strip is covered.

7. To finish, place the strip on the cutting mat with the paper side up, and trim away any fabric that sticks out beyond the edge of the paper.

8. Remove the paper when the entire quilt top has been set together. Crease the paper at the seamline to make it easier to tear and remove.

About the Authors

The Green Country Quilter's Guild in Tulsa, Oklahoma, can be credited for bringing together Linda Jenkins and Becky Goldsmith. Their friendship developed while they worked together on many guild projects and through a shared love for appliqué. This partnership led to the birth of Piece O' Cake Designs in 1994 and survived Linda's move to Pagosa Springs, Colorado, while Becky headed for Sherman, Texas.

Linda owned and managed a beauty salon before she started quilting. Over the years she developed a fine eye for color as a hair colorist and makeup artist. Becky's degree in interior design and many art classes provided a perfect background for quilting. Linda and Becky have shown many quilts and have won numerous awards. Together they make a dynamic quilting duo and love to teach other quilters the joys of appliqué.

In the fall of 2002 Becky and Linda joined the C&T Publishing family, where they continue to produce wonderful books and patterns.

Other Favorites by Piece O' Cake Designs

*The Appliqué Sampler
Learn to Appliqué the
Piece O' Cake Way!*

*Once Upon a Season
Nine Appliquéd and
Pieced Quilts, Celebrating
Every Season*

*Slice of Christmas
7 Sparkling Christmas
Projects*

*Contemporary Classics
in Plaids & Stripes
9 Projects from
Piece O' Cake Designs*

Index

Projects

Useful Information

For More Information

Write for a Free Catalog:
C&T Publishing, Inc.
P.O. Box 1456, Lafayette, CA 94549
800-284-1114
email: ctinfo@ctpub.com
website: www.ctpub.com

Resources

Vellum
For paper piecing and string piecing
Simple Foundations Translucent Vellum Paper
30 sheets per package, 8 ½" x 11"
Ask for it at your local quilt shop or order directly
from C&T Publishing at 800-284-1114.

Quilting Supplies
Cotton Patch Mail Order
3404 Hall Lane, Dept CTB, Lafayette, CA 94549
800-835-4418   925-283-7883
email: quiltusa@yahoo.com
website: www.quiltusa.com

*Note: Fabrics used in the quilts shown may not be
currently available since fabric manufacturers keep
most fabrics in print for only a short time.*